APERTURE

How do you image a culture? How does a culture image itself—especially one as splintered as Ireland's in the time of "the Troubles?" "Ireland: A Troubled Mirror" offers provocative responses to these questions—through photographs made by Irish and non-Irish photographers over the last thirty years. Images capturing the archetypal, mythical, and the everyday Ireland, North and South, are enhanced by illuminating essays and the trenchant, metaphorical poetry of Paul Muldoon.

Taking its title from a phrase in a poem by Yeats, "Ireland: A Troubled Mirror" counterpoises and reflects the Ireland of tourism and that of the international news media—the former, in the words of Tanya Kiang, consisting of "check-as-appropriate…green fields/blue skies/thatched cottages/donkeys/red-haired children," and the latter comprising "a formulaic list of gray streets/children/guns/soldiers' rubble" that has for a quarter-century served to represent the six counties of northeast Ireland.

The tension between these ideas of imaging also mirrors the argument according to which certain photographic battle lines have long been drawn—with the colorized postcard art of John Hinde coming down firmly on the side of formalism, and the black-and-white tableaus of bloody confrontations between police, youths, and rival political groups captured by the photojournalism of Don McCullin, Jim Tynan, and others. In these pages, you will witness how some new Irish photography synthesizes both approaches—and a range of others—in remarkably original, paradoxical works.

This issue of Aperture seeks to convey a sense of politics as they are embedded in the land, revealed in images of people and places, reflecting the bifurcated Irish political identity. In Ed Kashi's captivating documentary studies; in Paul Seawright's elegiac color landscapes of political violence; in the vibrant, crowded sitcomlike depictions of Irish family life by Anthony Haughey; in Sean Hillen's fantastical British/Irish photomontages of a mythical village called LondonNewry; in "The Rules of the Women of Ireland," Amelia Stein's mock altarpiece of a naked bride performing the rites of obedience, as well as in the art of many other superb talents—there surges a fierce energy, a friction between the lush and the stark.

This energy imbues the sequence of images with a rugged lyricism, borne along in interweaving poems from Paul Muldoon, which were selected by the poet to complement the photographs. Articles by Artforum senior editor David Frankel, who spent much of his boyhood in Ireland and England before moving to America, and by Tanya Kiang, editor of Circa, the preeminent Irish arts journal, offer insights into photography in Ireland and the persistence of "Irishness" among emigrants to the United States.

As we go to press in early December of 1993, newspapers report that Britain, the Irish Republic, and representatives of the Nationalist and Loyalist North may soon sit at the same table to begin discussing a resolution to the island's complex agony. Whatever the outcome of this pivotal historical moment, perhaps "Ireland: A Troubled Mirror" will impart a richer understanding of the struggle as it impacts on daily life—and of photography's unique ability to give visceral expression to abstract emotions and ideas—its ability, in short, to image a culture.

CONTENTS

Josef Koudelka, *Ireland*, 1972

When Oisin came back
  to Ireland
After three hundred years
On one of those
  enchanted islands
Somewhere in the
  Western Seas,

He thought nothing
  of dismounting
From his enchanted steed
To be one again with
  the mountains,
The bogs and the little fields.

There and then he began
  to stoop,
His hair, and all his teeth,
  fell out,
A mildewed belt,
  a rusted buckle.
The clays were heavy,
  black or yellow,
Those were the colours
  of his boots.
And I know something
  of how he felt.

—PAUL MULDOON

Jim Tynan, *Allihies*,
County Cork, 1982

LULL

I've heard it argued in some quarters
That in Armagh they mow the hay
With only a week to go to Christmas,
That no one's in a hurry

To save it, or their own sweet selves.
Tomorrow is another day,
As your man said on the
   Mount of Olives.
The same is held of County Derry.

Here and there up and down
   the country
There are still houses where the fire
Hasn't gone out in a century.

I know that eternal interim;
I think I know what they're
   waiting for
In Tyrone, Fermanagh,
   Down and Antrim.

—P.M.

Brad Temkin, *Jim McKillop, Patric Magee,*
Alex O'Hara, and Denis McKillop, Glendum,
County Antrim, North Ireland, 1991

Martin Parr,
*Glenbergh
Races*,
County Kerry,
1982

Philip Jones Griffiths,
British Soldier, Derry,
North Ireland, 1973

Pages 12–13:
Don McCullin,
*Confrontation in
the Bogside,*
Derry, 1971

11

THE POST-COLONIAL BOY

BY DAVID FRANKEL

> Politics is happening inside these landscapes, and painful politics at that. And contemporary people live here…. In images like these the land vomits itself up; it rejects the identity fashioned for it—or the identity fashioned from it, and from its past.

Not long ago I left a New York dinner party in a temper before the coffee was served. The talk had turned to Ireland.

I was a little startled to discover myself outside on the street. It wasn't that I hadn't known my attachment to Ireland—born here, part Irish-American, I lived there as a child and visit most years. Utterly unexpected was the degree of feeling, the depth of sensitivity to a conversation I saw as slighting—my feet got me out of there before I'd decided to leave.

So it may go among emigrants. (Although, again, it is a little startling to think of oneself as an emigrant, emigration being naturalized as the Irish condition.) But we are just as likely to have the opposite experience, stunned not by closeness but by distance. As a teenager in London, where my family moved when I was ten, I nursed my Irish accent even as it faded. London was a cold place, Ireland a warm memory; though eventually you might have thought I'd grown up somewhere east of Ireland but west of Wales (somewhere impossible, that is), I believed I spoke as an Irishman and, when I was sixteen or seventeen, told a Dublin friend so. She burst out laughing. My accent came from a place that doesn't exist.

Which is appropriate, really, and okay. It's not as if the place you remember is ever the place that is. That's memory's given.

What was this place I remember, which doesn't exist? In Dublin in the fifties and early sixties, a man and a horse delivered milk in the morning in glass bottles. There were few cars and many bikes. The city was quiet, safe: at seven or eight, when I wanted to go to a bookshop, I took a bus across town by myself. (I got lost, it was terrifying.) We played in the street all day, unwatched.

Dublin was small enough that it seemed you could be outside it—in the mountains, by the sea—in twenty minutes wherever you were. We lived in the mountains for a while, in a stone-floored cottage, now a stable. It stood at the edge of a field of dock and nettle, cows and a bull. Once a toad got into the scullery, leaping as high as my head. (I was little.) The cottage was the gatehouse of an old Anglo-Irish estate; every year there was a hunt—horses, dogs, a crowd, red coats against the green, supposedly a fox. The field looked all the way across Dublin to the bay.

In the summers we'd go to the West. The romance of names, as we drove: Kildare, Galway, Connemara, Mayo, Achill. Here there were even fewer cars; people used donkeys for hauling and riding. On Sundays they might go to church in a horse and trap. They let me come to the *ceilidh*, a wild party in a pub. Donkeys wandered the beaches. Lobsters crawled the floor of the hotel. A house we stayed in was lit, elegantly, by gas lamps; and one day Mr. Thornton's hat blew off, into the sea.

Needless to say, the sky was blue and clear, the sun hot. The humidity, low. (In fact I do remember dramatic summer sunburns.)

Collecting Turf from the Bog, Connemara, County Galway—how different is that from my Ireland? A picture postcard by John Hinde, it does, after all, have a donkey in it. Notice the reds: Hinde loved red. He thought it caught the tourist's eye on the display racks. When he photographed London, he'd make sure a London bus was in the frame. Here he must have liked the girl's shirt, and both children's hair, which may have been why he picked them.

Or maybe Martin Parr's *Horseracing,* Glenbeigh, County Kerry. No donkey. Horse.

Perhaps Parr remembered the Synge play *The Playboy of the Western World,* which turns on a horse race along a western beach. The Irish have a myth of the West, and Synge, with Yeats and Lady Gregory and other writers of his time (late nineteenth, early twentieth century), is partly responsible for it. *The Playboy* is a poetical piece, crafted, witty, poignant. It might seem to be what art historians talking about painting call a genre work: the colorful common people, their rude courtships, their rowdy pleasures, their folklore, their sympathy with nature. All

(continued on page 32)

Axel Grünewald,
Untitled,
Belfast, 1988

Rod Tuach, *County Galway*, 1983

OUR LADY OF ARDBOE

I

Just there, in a corner of the whin-field,
Just where the thistles bloom.
She stood there as in Bethlehem
One night in nineteen fifty-three or four.

The girl leaning over the half-door
Saw the cattle kneel, and herself knelt.

II

I suppose that a farmer's youngest daughter
Might, as well as the next, unravel
The winding road to Christ's navel.

Who's to know what's knowable?
Milk from the Virgin Mother's breast,
A feather off the Holy Ghost?
The fairy thorn? The holy well?

Our simple wish for there being more to life
Than a job, a car, a house, a wife—
The fixity of running water.

For I like to think, as I step these acres,
That a holy well is no more shallow
Nor plummetless that the pools of Shiloh,
The fairy thorn no less true than the Cross.

III

Mother of our Creator, Mother of our Saviour,
Mother most amiable, Mother most admirable.
Virgin most prudent, Virgin most venerable,
Mother inviolate, Mother undefiled.

And I walk waist-deep among purples and gold
With one arm as long as the other.

—P. M.

Above: Tony O'Shea, *Travelers*, Dublin, Tallaght, 1986

Below: Sarah Cully, *Altar Girls*, Ballyfermot, County Dublin, 1992

Above: Ed Kashi, At the Strandtown Social Club in East Belfast, a mostly Loyalist crowd kicks up its heels, 1989

Below: Tony O'Shea, *Dublin Rock Concert*, vacant lot, Parnell Street, 1988

Pages 19–21: Anthony Haughey, from the "Home" series, 1991

Joel Sternfeld,
Looking Across the
Corrib River to
Claddagh Quay,
Galway, 1985

Alen MacWeeney,
*Leahy's and
Horses Leaping a
Wall*, Loughrea,
County Galway,
1984

WHY BROWNLEE LEFT

Why Brownlee left,
   and where he went,
Is a mystery even now.
For if a man should have
   been content
It was him;
   two acres of barley,
One of potatoes,
   four bullocks,
A milker, a slated
   farmhouse.
He was last seen
   going out to plough
On a March morning,
   bright and early.

By noon Brownlee
   was famous;
They had found
   all abandoned, with
The last rig unbroken,
   his pair of black
Horses, like man and wife,
Shifting their weight
   from foot to
Foot, and gazing into
   the future.

—P. M.

Alen MacWeeney,
Islander Scything
Corn Field, Inishmore
Aran Island, 1985

27

Alen MacWeeney,
*Farmer's Gateway with
Model Farmhouse and
Plow*, County Down, 1985

All postcards by John Hinde

Top: *Collecting Turf from the Bog*,
Connemara, County Galway, 1960

Middle: *Sunset over the River Liffey
and Four Courts*, Dublin, 1965

Bottom: *Medieval Banquet*,
Bunratty Castle, County Clare, 1965

In the summers we'd go to the West. The romance of names, as we drove: Kildare, Galway, Connemara, Mayo, Achill. Here there were even fewer cars; people used donkeys for hauling and riding. On Sundays they might go to church in a horse and trap. They let me come to the *ceilidh*, a wild party in a pub. Donkeys wandered the beaches. Lobsters crawled the floor of the hotel.

Top: *Nelson's Pillar*, O'Connell Street and Bridge, Dublin, 1963

Middle: *Kissing the Blarney Stone*, Blarney Castle, County Cork, 1970

Bottom: *An Irish Donkey*, 1970

(continued from page 14)

this is in the play, but Synge didn't mean to condescend. The Irish were getting ready to free themselves, finally, of the British occupation. (Having lasted centuries, it ended fifteen or so years after Synge wrote.) Who would they be, what would they be, on their own? *The Playboy of the Western World* says: Ireland has its own life. Its richness is clear from its speech; and it has nothing to do with England. The play's story (a son tries to kill his father, who won't die) may be allegorically suggestive, but the crucial public issue of the time—the relationship with Britain—isn't discussed.

Martin Parr, *Crazy Prices Supermarket*, Ballyman, Dublin, 1986

The Irish myth of the West is a kind of reverse of the American one: here, a West imagined as vacant, waiting; in Ireland, a West once full of people. (Even after the nineteenth-century famines and emigrations began emptying it out, the government called it the "Congested Districts.") In the American myth the West's first peoples are at worst hostile, at best inconsequential; in the Irish, they're the guardians of the country's language, of its oral history, of its Gaelic self. Here, as we receive the myth, watch the movie, we move west with invaders from the east, into an open space of opportunity. There we are penned in from the east, in a land at once stronghold and prison.

The myths aren't really opposite: it's just that the American myth is told from the invaders' point of view. In American terms, the Irish are the Indians.

On a New York terrace, a woman from Virginia told me she had visited Ireland once, as a tourist, and had loved it. I asked her why: "Because it's tragic," she said, "and because of their sense of history. It reminds me of the South." Ireland is like the American West, Ireland is like the American South: Ireland is very like a whale. But what the South and the West share, and share with Ireland, is a history of bitter struggle over the land, incompletely resolved, and vividly alive in the mind.

On Inishbofin, an island off far western Galway, a man pointed out to me, a child then, a rock offshore in the harbor. On "the priest's rock," he told me, three hundred years before, Protestant soldiers from the east had chained a Catholic priest at low tide, then watched as the water rose. Elsewhere, "the priest's leap": the priest had jumped off a cliff rather than be taken alive. I can't say that it happened, can't say that it didn't. What's clear is the attitude: landscape and history are one, and are powerful.

Imagine walking Gettysburg with a Civil War nut—but this was just a rock in the ocean, and someone passing by.

So Paul Seawright, when he photographs a dumping ground for "sectarian murder," makes sure you can see the dolmen in the field, and the grass. The captions tell you you're looking at a tourist spot, a beauty spot. Or he shows you a swell of hillside, a clutch of flowers, a stretch of sky. The bodies have already been taken away. Paul Graham photographs a townscape as a kind of flattened, thin version of the picturesque, in fact a dismal pictorial failure—the hills that might shape the photo way off in the distance, everything flat, no one around, in the foreground the graffiti, in Hinde red: BEWARE. Politics is happening inside these landscapes, and painful politics at that. And contemporary people live here, perhaps in the crowded, specific clutter of the family lovingly photographed by Anthony Haughey; or in the brutal circumstances of the northern conflict, or perhaps as mohawk-wearing sightseers enjoying the sun on a fishing-village pier. In images like these the land vomits itself up; it rejects the identity fashioned for it—or the identity fashioned from it, and from its past.

Joyce, famously, wrote of forging in the smithy of his soul the uncreated conscience of his race. The line is often taken to describe what the artist does, anywhere, but the time of its writing, midway through the fifteen years between *The Playboy* and independence, suggests another reading: in the difficult, contested expulsion of the colonial, the need to build something for nation, people, to be. As it turned out, the foundations available were history and land—a history part recent, part ancient, part mythic, a landscape of striking pictorial passages. Social fact—the ground largely rural, the economy largely agrarian, industry largely gutted or stillborn under British rule—channeled the construction. The product: a contender in the marketplace of modern tourism.

The remark, though true, is cheap. It implies an easy kind of transaction. Not long ago at a Dublin dinner party, telling Irish friends I was on my way to a vacation in the West, I saw them exchange a quick look. The Irish are well aware of the tensions of their modern state. All the way through this book, you watch the argument. □

Elliott Erwitt, *Ireland*, 1963

Robert Ballagh, *Reads, Parliament Street*, 1980

Robert Ballagh, *The River Liffey below Butt Bridge*, 1980

Victor Sloan, *Stay Out*, Craigavon, 1991

Victor Sloan, *Route 3*, County Armagh, 1991

THE CENTAURS

I can think of William of Orange, / Prince of gasworks-wall and gable-end.
A plodding, snow-white charger / On the green, grassy slopes of the Boyne,
The milk-cart swimming against the current

Of our own backstreet. Hernan Cortes / Is mustering his cavalcade on the pavement,
Lifting his shield like the lid of a garbage-can. / His eyes are fixed on a river of Aztec silver,
He whinnies and paws the earth

For our amazement. And Saul of Tarsus, / The stone he picked up once has grown into a hoof.
He slings the saddle-bags over his haunches, / Lengthening his reins, loosening his girth,
To thunder down the long road to Damascus.

—P. M.

Victor Sloan, *Walk 10 Lurgan*, County Armagh, 1985/1991

Victor Sloan, *Sham Fight*, Scarva, County Down, 1992

Above: Axel Grünewald, *Untitled*, Belfast, 1988

Bottom: Philip Jones Griffiths, *Loyalist with Sword*, North Ireland, Derry, 1973

Philip Jones Griffiths, *British Soldier*, 1973

Predictable as the gift of the gab
or a drop of the craythur
he noses round the six foot deep
crater.
Oblivious to their Landrover's
olive-drab
and the Burgundy berets
of a snatch-squad of Paratroopers.
Gallogly, Gollogly,
otherwise known as Golightly,
otherwise known as Ingoldsby,
otherwise known as English,
gives forth one low cry of anguish
and agrees to come quietly.

They have bundled him into the cell
for a strip-
search.
He perches
on the balls of his toes, my, my,
with his legs spread
till both his instep arches
fall.
He holds himself at arm's
length from the brilliantly Snowcem-ed
wall, a game bird
hung by its pinion tips
till it drops, in the fullness of time,
from the mast its colours are nailed to.

—P. M.

41

Ná clois a gcloisfir.

Ná feic a bhfeicfir.

DON'T HEAR WHAT YOU HEAR

DON'T SEE WHAT YOU SEE

Amelia Stein, *The Four Rules of the Women of Ireland*, 1992

Ná scaoil faoi t'onáil é.

Ná scaoil id'spaŕán é.

DON'T BREATHE A WORD OF IT

DON'T LET HIM INTO YOUR PUSS

Philip Jones Griffiths, *British Soldier*, Derry, North Ireland, 1973

little did I think that S____ would turn to me one night:
'The only Saracen I know's a Saracen tank
with a lion rampant on its hood;

from Aghalane to Artigarvan to Articlave
the Erne and the Foyle and the Bann must run red';
that must have been the year Twala's troops were massacred.

—P. M.

Dana Tynan, *Lavery's Pub*, Belfast, 1989

Brian, a Loyalist youth from Tiger's Bay in Belfast, prepares for another day with his nighttime protection safely within reach. He lives within two hundred yards of a Nationalist estate that staunchly backs the IRA.

Making a flame-thrower using hairspray might seem violent and destructive, but to Brian it's just another way to fill an empty day.

Not fighting, but "playing" (according to Brian) with girlfriend Sharon, 16.

Brian's first time at a disco. Fearful that Nationalists might show up looking for a fight, this night he goes with a group of his buddies.

All photographs by Ed Kashi, from the "Life of Brian" series, 1989

Seán Hillen, *Newry Gagarin #12*, 1992

THE SIGHTSEERS

My father and mother, my brother and sister
and I, with uncle Pat, our dour best-loved uncle,
had set out that Sunday afternoon in July
in his broken-down Ford

not to visit some graveyard—one died of shingles,
one of fever, another's knees turned to jelly—
but the brand-new roundabout at Ballygawley,
the first in mid-Ulster.

Uncle Pat was telling us how the B-Specials
had stopped him one night somewhere near Ballygawley
and smashed his bicycle

and made him sing the Sash and curse the Pope of Rome.
They held a pistol so hard against his forehead
there was still the mark of an O when he got home.

—P. M.

All photographs by Paul Seawright, from the "Sectarian Murder" series, 1988

Tuesday 30th January 1973 *"The car travelled to a deserted tourist spot known as the Giants Ring. The 14 year old boy was made to kneel on the grass verge, his anorak was pulled over his head, then he was shot at close range, dying instantly."*

Sunday July 9, 1972, "*The 31 year old man was found under some bushes in Cavehill Park. He had been shot dead. The police believe it to have been a sectarian murder.*"

Monday 3rd July 1972 *"The man had left home to buy some drink; he was found later on waste ground nearby. He had been badly beaten and it seems he had been tied to a chair with barbed wire before being shot through the head."*

Friday May 25, 1973, "*The murdered man's body was found lying at the Giants Ring beauty spot, once used for pagan rituals. It has now become a regular location for sectarian murder.*"

Tuesday, April 3, 1973, "*Late last night a 28 year old man disappeared from a pub. It wasn't until this morning that his body was found abandoned in a quiet park on the coast.*"

PLAYING THE GREEN CARD

CONTEMPORARY PHOTOGRAPHY IN IRELAND

BY TANYA KIANG

Paul Graham, *Graffiti Ballysillian Estate*, Belfast, 1986

The photographs many young Irish people would most like to see are not shown in galleries, museums, newspapers, or magazines. The sought-after photographs are those small, rigorously disciplined "identity shots" laminated onto every green card. Such photographs can open doors to a world that appears richer, more vibrant. Lacking context and particular histories, these images remain unruffled by the complexities of lived experience. They can say, quite simply, "This is me"—and say it as though that were sufficient. With an enviable authority, the identity shot offers a kind of "identity degree zero."

The identity shot is accompanied by a fingerprint and a signature. Thus, the green card marshals all three representatives from the semiotic canon: the image, a sign by resemblance, the fingerprint, a sign by physical causation, the signature, a sign by linguistic convention. The complete signifying battery is mobilized in an attempt to nail down a denotation of identity.

Regulations governing the identity shot are issued by the U.S. Immigration and Naturalization Service in a blotchy photocopy giving examples of "dos" and "don'ts." The image must be clearly lit, crisply focused, of uniform contrast, and of exacting dimensions. It must show the full face, head turned slightly and hair drawn back to reveal the right ear.

Apparently, the ear is one of the most distinctive features of a person: with its whorls and spirals, it is something of a fingerprint. I must confess to a fascination with ears. In the last century, an art connoisseur by the name of Morelli found that minute scrutiny of the way ears were painted was one of the surest methods of identifying—not the depicted people—but the artist. It's as if the ears gave the game away, gave the painter up. It might appear that no such turning of the representational tables can occur in a photograph. Yet in a sense the real maker of the identity shot is clearly revealed. It's not the person of the photographer, or the lidless eye of the photomat, but the various institutions of state who *author*-ize them. As the rigor of the guidelines indicate, these images are constructions framed for the official gaze of the U.S. Department of Justice.

On the face of it—pardon the pun—these identity shots are hardly what you would call "real" photographs. Where they stop, "real" photographs begin. Where one reduces and desiccates the complexities of personal, cultural, and national identities, the other elaborates and enriches them. But they share one important characteristic with the vast majority of other images of Ireland. They are images *of*, not *for* the people living here.

The dominant images of Ireland—whether by Irish or visiting photographers—are constructed to meet the criteria of two industries: tourism and the international news media. Because both produce for markets outside of the country, the images in circulation are mainly addressed to an international audience, or to specific market niches of it. As with the green card's reduction of the complexities of personal identity, the romanticized landscapes that are the staple of the tourist genre offer a check-as-appropriate combination of green fields/blue skies/thatched cottages/donkeys/red-haired children. In a similarly reductive vein, media reportage of the Northern Ireland conflict over the last twenty-five years has operated with a formulaic checklist of gray streets/children/guns/soldiers/rubble in an elision of the complexity of human events.

The dominance of these two representational regimes points to the nascent state of independent photography in Ireland. Here, the small size of the Irish market poses obvious obstacles to the expensive business of making, publishing, and distributing photographs. Without a ready commercial market, public funding is necessary, and yet historically, there has been little interest in photography as a medium of cultural exploration and critique. During the decades after Ireland gained its political independence, appeal was made to literature, drama, music, and landscape painting for cultural definition and the development of a national self-image. Insular and backward-looking, a narrowly nationalistic "traditional" Irish culture was constructed in a process that largely eclipsed the contemporaneous validation of photography and other forms of Modernist experimentation that were underway elsewhere. It was not until the late seventies that the state awarded a small bursary to an independent

(continued on page 61)

Above: Seán Hillen, *The Virgin appears to Her Majesty, Security Forces Investigate*, 1987

Below: Seán Hillen, *Trouble in Paradise #1*, 1993

Steven Shortt,
*Dead
Policemen*,
Belfast, 1986

James Nachtwey,
Irish Nationalist
demonstrators hijacked
a car, parked it in the
entranceway to a British
fort, and set it on fire.
When the British
dispatched an armored
front-loader to remove
the flaming barricade,
demonstrators attacked it
with petrol bombs. 1981

Among the blue flowers
  of the flax a linnet
  sang out 'Lundy'

at the implications
  of that bleach-
  green. 'It was merely a
  figure of speech.'

'Call it what you like.
  The grey skies of
  an Irish Republic

are as nothing compared
  to this blue dome.'
He tailed off
  over the flax-dam

to return with a charm
  of goldfinches
who assailed me with
  their 'Not an inch'

and their 'No', and
  yet again, 'No'.
As they asperged me
  with kerosene

I recognized the voice of
  Sir Edward Carson;
'Bid me strike a match
  and blow.'

—P. M.

Donna DeCesare,
National Front (neo-Nazi)
Supporter at Loyalist
Demonstration, Derry,
North Ireland, 1986

(continued from page 54)

photographer and the first gallery specializing in photographic exhibitions was established.

Now, there are signs of further development: the Gallery of Photography will shortly be moving to a new Centre for Photography in Dublin; and a group called Photoworks North has recently been formed in Belfast. These organizations have done much to foster critical photographic work, although the urban middle class remains underrepresented, as does work from specific feminist perspectives.

In a more general sense, these organizations have difficult tasks ahead. For, at best, it is simply unrealistic—and at worst, xenophobic—to believe in the indigenous growth of independent photographic practices in Ireland: to wish to hold back the "filthy tide," to push away the cameras until we invent our own vision. This is why it is important not to dismiss the clichéd representations on the grounds that they are *only* for tourists, *only* for others. Such a move would fall back on the tired opposition between the clichéd image and the "real" Ireland, lurking somewhere underneath it all. It would also overlook the fact that, unlike the case with the green card, the authority of both the news media and the tourist industry is met with widespread skepticism, and the images they construct are therefore more open to critical readings.

The reaction in Dublin to a recent exhibition of photographs by John Hinde and the John Hinde Studios is a case in point. The sentimental, highly colorized postcard images made mainly during the sixties were greeted like old friends. People became animated, stories were told. It was accepted that the sky was an impossible blue and the foliage in the foreground would return to the bag of props in the photographer's van. The artifice and the stage-management of the photographs were understood (so much so that the short texts and anecdotal comments that accompanied the images were a bit like having a joke explained).

But just as viewers could "see through" the images, they were also aware of—and unsettled by—the nostalgia they prompted for an era of optimism when, as one commentator put it "ordinary people had the money and jobs to go on holidays." It's the sense of recognition that interests me. It is not just that the images spoke to people's experience of holidaying in Ireland. It goes further. They recognized something of themselves in them, for the tourist gaze is an integral, if very problematic, part of Irish culture.

To some, the projection of Ireland as a place steeped in past traditions, a backward, premodern, rural society with quaint, friendly people, is seen as a continuation of the negative colonial stereotypes of the Irish. In this light, the tourist gaze is "eye-level" with the old colonialist gaze; retarding and complicating the construction of a "modern," "postcolonial" self-image. Yet it might also be argued that the tourist image is knowingly constructed to meet the expectations of the canonical tourist in Ireland—the roots-seeking returned emigrant. For the immigrant populations of North America and the wider Irish diaspora, Ireland becomes an external, fixed, and unitary point of origin and return: it carries the heavy cultural loading of "home." As one critic noted, "In John Hinde's Irish postcards, there is an uneasy feeling that we are getting a last glimpse of a world that is lost. It is as if the emigrant's break with the past has been internalized within Irish culture, forming its popular image of itself."

By contrast, the dominant imagery of "the Troubles" in the North reveals no internal temporal fissure, no problematic nostalgia. Indeed, the in-and-out, quick-hit approach of the international photojournalist has been criticized from many points of view: for simplifying, for glorifying, for victimizing, and, in the words of Margaret Thatcher, for lending "the oxygen of publicity to terrorists." Thatcher's slogan heralded the censorship in the United Kingdom of spokespersons for proscribed organizations such as the IRA. This was passed by the British government in 1988, while a similar ban has been in place in the Republic of Northern Ireland since 1974. The censorship applies directly to broadcasting organizations, but its effects have spilled over to the print media. Now, there seems to be less photographic coverage of Northern Ireland in the press. After twenty-five years of the Troubles, few people are interested in trying to make sense of what is going on in Northern Ireland: the situation appears intractable, and many simply wish "the Northern problem" would just go away.

In these difficult circumstances, it has been left up to the small number of photographers using other means of reaching an audience to try to document and explore what passes for "normal" life in the North. In 1983, one commentator could make the claim that "Loyalist paramilitaries, Orange demonstrations, religion, housing, unemployment, and the constant presence of the security forces in the shape of camps, armored cars, helicopters, searches of people and houses . . . are simply not seen." In the interim, many of these neglected areas have been addressed. Whether it be the disciplined understatement of Paul Graham, or the humanist documentary of Ed Kashi, independent photography from Northern Ireland is united in presenting a more inclusive vision and in resisting the familiar spectacle of violence as represented in the news media.

Much of this new work shows a distrust of the straight image. For example, Victor Sloan's authorial interventions choreograph an image in ways that owe as much to the aural as to the visual environment. By contrast, Willie Doherty's work is drained of authorial presence: he appropriates the deadpan, controlling vision of the surveillance camera, unsettling its brutal denotation by keen positioning of short, resonant text. Distrust of the certainties of the dominant visual transitions is also manifest in Seán Hillen's use of photomontage. He inserts signs of the Northern conflict into the city of London, or transports icons of London to his hometown Newry, in a reflection of the dislocations of the emigrant's experience. LondoNewry, his reconstituted mythical town, corrodes the unities of "place" and of "home," refracting them into disparate geographical, political, and cultural elements that fit together only with the friction of humor.

Such images offer an alternative to the reliance on stereotypes of our own making, stereotypes that insist on a spurious "Irishness." In taking on board a wider critical vision, and through engaging and questioning uncertainties, perhaps now Irish identities need no longer conform to a made-to-order image. Perhaps now they can be played by ear. □

Willie Doherty, *The Other Side*, Derry, 1988

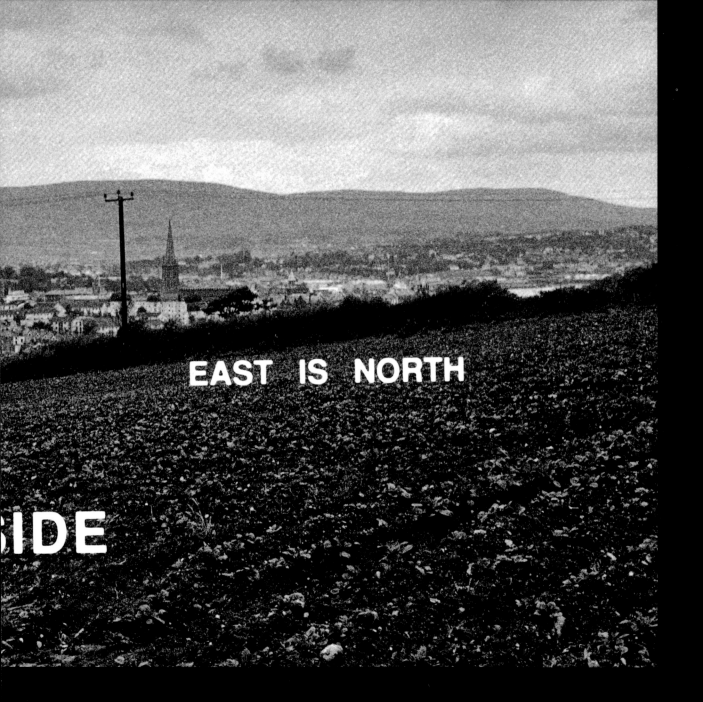

EAST IS NORTH

SIDE

THE BOUNDARY COMMISSION

You remember that village where the border ran
Down the middle of the street,
With the butcher and baker in different states?
Today he remarked how a shower of rain

Had stopped so cleanly across Golightly's lane
It might have been a wall of glass
That had toppled over. He stood there, for ages,
To wonder which side, if any, he should be on.

He is going to put his foot down
on a patch of waste ground
along the Stranmillis embankment
when he gets wind
of their impromptu fire.
The air above the once-sweet stream
is aquarium-
drained.
And six, maybe seven, skinheads
have formed a quorum
round a burnt-out heavy-duty tyre.
So intent on sniffing glue
they may not notice Gallogly,
or, if they do, are so far gone.

Three miles west as the crow flies
an all-night carry-out
provides the cover
for an illegal drinking club.
While the bar man unpacks a crate
of Coca-Cola,
one cool customer
takes on all comers in a video game.
He grasps what his two acolytes
have failed to seize.
Don't they know what kind of take-aw
this is, the glipes?
Vietmanese. Viet-ma-friggin'-knees.
He drops his payload of napalm.

—P. M

Philip Jones Griffiths, *British Soldier*, North Ireland, Derry, 1973

Above: Abbas, *Children Playing War Games in Back Streets of Derry*, 1972

Below: Jim Tynan, Sean Downes lies mortally wounded, shot by the Royal Ulster Constabulary at a Nationalist rally, 1984

The U.D.R. corporal had come
  off duty
to be with his wife
while the others set about
a follow-up search.
When he tramped out
  just before twelve
to exercise the greyhound
he was hit by a single high-velocity
shot.
You could, if you like, put your fist
in the exit wound
in his chest.
He slumps
in the spume of his own
  arterial blood
like an overturned paraffin lamp.

Gallogly lies down in the sheugh
to munch
through a Beauty of
Bath. He repeats himself, Bath,
under his garlic-breath.
Sheugh, he says. Sheugh.
He is finding that first 'sh'
increasingly difficult to manage.
Sh-leeps. A milkmaid sinks
her bare foot
to the ankle
in a simmering dung hill
and fills the slot
with beastlings for him to drink.

—P. M.

Don McCullin,
Confrontation in the
Bogside, Derry, 1971

Axel Grünewald, *Untitled*, Belfast, 1988

...NIEL LENNON
    10-8-1976 I.R.A.
FRANCIS FITZSIMMONS
    16-10-1976 I.R.A.
.FF CAPT JOS.SURGENOR
    16-10-1976 I.R.A.
.FF CAPT PAUL MARLOWE
    16-10-1976 - I.R.A.
...RE DRUMM, ASSASSINATED
    28-10-1976 SINN FEIN
..DIE DOLAN 9-2-1975 Cm.ban.
..THOS. TOLAN
    27-7-1977 - I.R.A.
.L Mc WILLIAMS
    9-8-1977 - NA.FE.
.EVOR McKIBBIN
    17-4-1977 - NA.FE.
..DENIS BROWN
    21-6-1978 - I.R.A.
..JAMES MULVENNA
    21-6-1978 - I.R.A.
..JACKIE MAILEY
    21-6-1978 - I.R.A.
..FRANK DONNELLY
    6-1-1979 - I.R.A.
...RENCE MONTGOMERY
    ...-1979 I.R.A.

ALEX GAMBLE, BALLYMONEY.
GEO. DICKSON, CRUMLIN.
SAMUEL DUNLOP, BALLYMONEY.
J. McILROY, BALLYCASTLE.
DAVID WOODS CONNOR
DAN ENGLISH.
HENRY HOLYWELL, BALLYMENA.
DOCTOR LYNN RANDALSTOWN
JAS. GRIFFIN, CULLYBACKEY
BARTHOLOMEW TEELING, LISBU...
A. HUNTER, CARRICKFERGUS.
D. PORTER,

AND ALL THEIR NOBLE UNKNOW...
DURING THE 1798 PERIOD AND W...
OR UNKNOWN GRAVES.

HANGED 1798 UNITED IRISHMEN
    1798
    1798 BALLYMONEY,
    1798 BALLYCASTLE
    1798
    1798
    1798 CARRICKFERGUS.
    1798
    1798
...RN. 1798 DUBLIN.
    KILLED 1803
    1803

...COMRADES WHO WERE KILLED.
...ERE BURIED IN COMMON

After drinking all night in a
  Sands Street shebeen
where a sailor played a melodeon
made from a merman's spine
I left by the back door of Muldoon's

(it might have been the Rotterdam)
on a Monday morning, falling in with
the thousands of shipyardmen
  who tramped
towards the front gates of Harland
  and Wolff.

The one-eyed foreman had strayed
  out of Homer;
'MacNeice? That's a Fenian name.'
As if to say, 'None of your sort,
  none of you

will as much as go for a
  rubber hammer
never mind chalk a rivet, never
  mind caulk a seam
on the quinquereme of Nineveh.'

—P. M.

Ed Kashi, *Samson and Goliath, the
Twin Towers of the Harland and
Wolff Shipyard*, East Belfast, 1988

Axel Grünewald, *Untitled*, Belfast, 1988

PEOPLE AND IDEAS

AN AUTOBIOGRAPHY, RICHARD AVEDON

By Glenn O'Brien

An Autobiography, *by Richard Avedon, published by Random House / Eastman Kodak Company, New York, 1993 ($100.00 hardcover).*

When I first heard the title I thought it appropriate for a monumental career retrospective. But when I paged through the book, autobiography took on a new meaning.

This is autobiography in the sense that we speak of when, facing death, our lives are said to flash before our eyes. The montage of images presented here has that kind of power and sweep, that kind of peculiar paralogic, that kind of full emotional and experiential spectrum.

The sequence is at times dreamlike; images are juxtaposed with the skewed logic of the unconscious. A trivial similarity becomes a profoundly open-ended connection. Spreads of two pictures are instant equations. Pictures are linked by accidents of posture or gesture. Sometimes by a visual pun. Sometimes the images confront one another. Sometimes they flow with rhythm and alliteration and assonance. This is not a linear logic, but images yaw, pitch, and roll through the nexus of the conscious and unconscious, oscillating into unexpected epiphanies, eliciting troubling reverberation.

Hollywood director Lewis Milestone peers through pursed eyes, cold as a lizard, on a left-hand page, while a serpentine Hispanic carny leers perversely with snake eyes on the right. W. H. Auden stands in a snow flurry opposite a naked man covered with a swarm of bees. Poets and lovers Allen Ginsberg and Peter Orlovsky stand naked next to Henry Kissinger, Secretary of State, naked only in his ambition, as polar opposites of male sexiness. Simone, a model, is shown in kooky Correges slitted sunglasses opposite Vice President Nelson Rockefeller's flesh-shrouded eyes. But through it all Richard Avedon never resorts to low irony. His pictures are never

setups. They are perfect accidents of the sort that befall artists prepared to receive them. He never takes a cheap shot. When he takes a shot, it's expensive.

Photographers have various degrees of interaction with their subjects. Some, like Winogrand, take only what is offered; some, like Weegee, covertly heighten reality; others, like most fashion photographers, arrange everything. Avedon employs all of those approaches, as a street photographer, a portraitist, and a fashion photographer. He's a master both in catching the flow and in creating it. There is a strong thread running through the work, a signature of vision. It's hard to pinpoint just what makes Avedon Avedon. Paging through *An Autobiography* I thought of the rhythm and blues song "Can I Get a Witness?"

Avedon is a compulsive witness. He wants to see everything and he does. In his photomat self-portrait he stares down the lens, rapt, hungry, fascinated, his big wide-open eyes like black holes that will let no matter escape. His portraits, like those of the Duke and Duchess of Windsor; Oscar Levant; the Generals of the Daughters of the American Revolution; and Gene Pitney, singer, with his manager, are all equally revelatory. Avedon is the perfect witness, able to elicit self-revelation from his subject.

The only text in this book is a brief introduction by Avedon. The book would have been purer, in a way, with no words to explain it. But the words are few and well chosen. The book is divided into three sections. Avedon says they "track the path of three crucial illusions" in his life. The first is the "illusion of laughter and a young man's discovery of the fine line between hilarity and panic." The second is about "the illusion of power." The third is "about the loss of all illusions."

The sections may seem somewhat arbitrary, but then, the artist is the arbiter. At first I was struck by the starkly and violently contrasted imagery of the third sec-

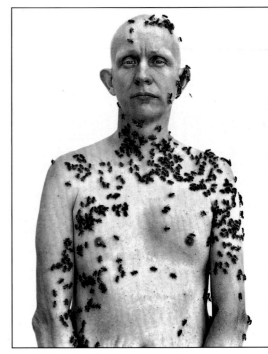

Ronald Fischer, beekeeper
Davis, California
May 9, 1981

Peter Orlovsky and Allen Ginsberg, poets
New York City
December 30, 1963

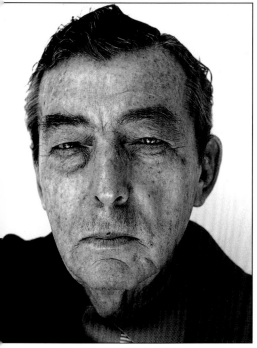

ewis Milestone, director
everly Hills, California
bril 10, 1972

Juan Patricio Lobato, carney
Rocky Ford, Colorado
August 23, 1980

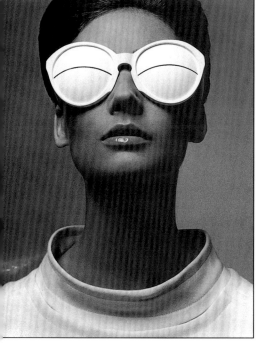

mone, model
aris
ebruary 4, 1965

Nelson Rockefeller,
Vice President of the United States
June 28, 1976

tion, which contains a much heavier dose of the grotesque than the rest of the book. Pictures of the semimummified dead from the catacombs of Palermo, and pictures of the lost-soul inmates of the East Louisiana State Hospital, and of disfigured Vietnamese napalm victims are found fairly early in the book, but later on these troubling presences increase in their frequency, abutting images of beauty and hope. It's as if an emotional rheostat has been turned up. At first this turn away from glamour and journalism toward more weighty and difficult material struck me as a bit heavy-handed, but finally, it works. The hand is heavy but it's graceful and true. It smacks you with transcendence. Hits you over the head with sublime dread. Avedon shows that there's not much difference between a cliché and a cosmic truth.

The most distinctly biographical elements of the book are Avedon's self-portraits and the portraits of his family: his father, whose startling portraits in the shadow of death are well known, his mother, his sister, his wives, children, and grandchildren. These are the simplest pictures in the book and, in a way, the most loaded, the most complex. We see Avedon's DNA in these pictures. We catch a glimpse of him in the fast-eroding skull of his father and in the eyes of his grandchildren. We wonder about the wives, three of them. Their portraits are iconographic mysteries blending accident and intent, innocence and experience, hope and fate.

In the end, *An Autobiography* is a book of the dead, which—Egyptian, Tibetan or modern—is a text for bringing the soul back to life, one way or another. The *Tibetan Book of the Dead* describes the progress of the soul after life, before rebirth, as a struggle against illusions, which is also Avedon's intention here. Perhaps this photographic book of the dead will help expedite the transit of souls through television limbos, image-overload *bardo*, and celebrity purgatories. In an age of unprecedented technology of illusion, Avedon's self-reckoning reveals the power of one person's vision, with control and finesse, to penetrate the illusory. As we witness a life, a very glamorous, intelligent, and thoroughly lived life, flashing before our eyes, we witness the process of witnessing, of seeing through what we see.

INDIAN CIRCUS, MARY ELLEN MARK

By Deborah Kayton

Indian Circus, *photographs by Mary Ellen Mark, foreword by John Irving, published by Chronicle Books, San Francisco, 1993 ($40.00 hardcover).*

With *Indian Circus*, Mary Ellen Mark continues her work documenting specific lives in difficult, self-contained environments to which gaining access is a challenge and communication crosses cultural boundaries. However, these photographs—of acrobats, clowns, contortionists, trainers, and animals of eighteen itinerant circuses throughout India—depict not only the resilience of spirit Mark has found in her past subjects, but a joyousness, a sense of pride, a rootedness, and an attuned physicality. Exceptional, if unfamous, performers respond without artifice to her camera. Mark took most of the seventy-four pictures during a six-month period in 1989–90; the others are as recent as 1992, and as distant as 1969. Her beautiful photographs are not big-top circus shots, but moments of rehearsal and backstage exis-

tence framed by tent poles and walls. Mark's is the India of enclosures, of caged Bombay prostitutes and hospices. And, reminiscent of her days photographing prom and Halloween goers, or shooting production stills—a Brando facing her off-screen—she again looks at the role and form of costume and makeup, but here the costume is the life, the makeup can be elaborate, and they are worn three times a day.

The performers exude a quiet, dignified self-possession, and one often feels a sense of their complicity with Mark. And, as in her work with street kids, *Indian Circus* uses lengthy quotations to emphasize the subjects' primacy. The photographs are akin to those of Western dancers or actors in rehearsal in their emphasis on the performer's trained body and carriage, and the implicit if not always present audience. The spare beauty of ritual preparation is heightened by the circumstances of nomadic life, cushioned by an evident sense of acceptance in self, family, and community.

Although the circus, imported to India from Europe in 1880, has a long history worldwide of employing children, the Indian circus is notable for the numbers of children of "outsiders." Yet in India, where children often are contractually signed over to the circus by their parents, cultural attitudes about childhood and the tradition of master-student relationships support the discipline of circus life. And it is in the photographs of children that the sense of dignity and movement becomes most poignant, juxtaposing their fragile vulnerability with extreme pliable gymnastic strength. Three small girls balance atop one another, their arms punctuating the air in Vs, their form casting a receding, sculptural shadow on the ground and wall which, given the photographer's perspective, throws all sense of geometry into the abstract. Mark catches another group jumping out of formation, midair a whir of tucked legs, as the central figure fixes on us, as present and directed as any adult. Elsewhere, the essential delicacy of freely floating arms—extended for both balance and panache—contrasts with this young girl's focused, earthbound concentration, as she precariously steadies a second child upside-down on her head, shifting her weight gracefully to one side. Throughout, as the girls contort, stretch into backbends, warm up, train, practice (be it atop each other or various objects), Mark sensitively angles her camera to accentuate the phenomenon of their bodies' flexibility.

The children's beauty is highlighted in Mark's photos of them at rest. Here they are just girls preening, sleeping. In *Famous Circus*, Calcutta, 1989, we follow the synchronized gesture of arms as two girls arc their backs in unison over the bedside to comb their hair, light shining on their translucent skin and white dresses against the darker floor. But sometimes the children look simply sad and small, especially when they are clowns, as when a brittle boy leans oddly near a huge tent while feeding some large cranes. Clowns embody a rich tradition in Indian myth and poetry, from the comic cripples of the medieval Tamil folk-drama, where their bodies represented a challenge to conventional form, to the clown of Sanskrit drama, who was funny—in appearance and action—despite himself, achieving status through self-parody. Mark's

Mary Ellen Mark, *Pinky, Sunita, and Ratna*, Great Royal Circus, Gujarat, 1989

clowns—many unusually proportioned, often dwarfs—comment as reflexive mirrors, spoilers of illusion, and counterpoints to the main action. Ram Pyare's S-shaped body bends sharply back at the knees, his arms hanging pendulously low, his hands clawlike. Dressed in a close-fitting, striped uniform with a jaunty cap, he seems to stand exposed, while a group of taller, loosely clad girls with conventionally beautiful physiques walk past him. The mythic clown, though lonely, is never alone, and these clowns always appear in the company of others.

Animals share an equally strong role and appear interchangeably with the human characters. Elephants play doctor, bears wear dresses, chimpanzees don their Sunday best. Plays on scale further articulate the tension in the images where, for example, twin dwarfs sport gorilla suits while holding a tiny dog. Indian circuses have added vultures, pelicans, and other animals to the spectacle, while retaining Western forms and popular music. In religious tradition, elephants bring fortune and monkeys are esteemed as messengers of Rama, but they are still work animals. As a chimp trainer says, "He is not my brother—he is my god and my stomach."

All lushly printed, the vibrant photographs stand out, but the book's design seems disjointed by random blank pages, and images are sequenced in a manner that feels neither organic nor coherent, although some individual juxtapositions work well. The overall jumble effectively portrays the chaotic yet ordered mixes of the circus, but makes the pacing awkward. Similarly, jumps between Mark's own comments and her quotations from the performers tend to chop the flow of each informative part of the text. And the limited number of photo sizes, coupled with an uninspired layout that ultimately emphasizes the white space, gives a static feeling to the progression. The design does, however, reinforce a frame that distances the viewer from the community's energy, a distance marked also by the inclusion at the book's opening of a photograph of crowds pressing to get into a performance. Mark's work brilliantly captures the dynamism of these disappearing traveling worlds, their lively contrasts and incongruities, making it clear why she considers the circus "a metaphor for everything that has always fascinated me visually."

Mary Ellen Mark, *Pinky, Sunita, and Ratna*, Great Royal Circus, Gujarat, 1989

Mary Ellen Mark, *Shanu and Tulsi Warming Up*, Bharat Circus, Utter Pradesh, 1989

CONTRIBUTORS

DAVID FRANKEL is senior editor at *Artforum* magazine, where he has worked for twelve years. His writing has appeared in *Artforum, Aperture, Kunstforum, African Arts, New York, Rolling Stone, The Berlitz Guide to New York City*, and elsewhere.

DEBORAH KAYTON directs Project ACRE, a dance and video program for teens in foster care throughout New York City. She also runs arts programs for the Educational Alliance and Legal Aid Society. She dances and choreographs throughout the nation, directs her own experimental dance company, and has taught multimedia work at Yale University and at New York's 92nd Street Y.

TANYA KIANG is editor of *Circa Art Magazine*, in Dublin.

PAUL MULDOON was born in 1951 in County Armagh, Northern Ireland, and studied in Armagh and at the Queen's University of Belfast. From 1973 to 1986 he worked in Belfast as a radio and television producer for the British Broadcasting Corporation. Since 1987 he has lived in the United States, where he has taught at Berkeley, Columbia, and the University of Massachusetts: he is now the director of the Creative Writing Program at Princeton.

He has produced several poetry collections, including *Selected Poems 1968–1986*, published by Ecco Press in 1987 and by Farrar, Straus and Giroux in 1993, and a new collection, *The Annals of Chile*, which will appear in the fall of 1994. He was also the editor of *The Faber Book of Contemporary Irish Poetry*, 1986.

GARY NICKARD is Director of Programs at Artist's Space in New York City and an artist involved with photography installation and mixed media. He was formerly Gallery Director for the Burden Gallery at Aperture and Associate Curator at the Alternative Museum, both in New York City. Previously he served as Executive and Artistic Director at CEPA in Buffalo, New York.

GLENN O'BRIEN is a Contributing Editor of *Details* and *Allure* magazines, and a regular writer for *Artforum*. He is also the Creative Director of Advertising for Barney's New York.

CREDITS

Unless otherwise noted, all photographs are courtesy of, and copyright by, the artist.

Front cover photograph by Karl Grimes; pp. 4–5 Jim Tynan, courtesy Impact Visuals; pp. 8–9 Martin Parr, courtesy Magnum Photos, New York; pp 10–11 Philip Jones Griffiths, courtesy Magnum Photos, New York; pp.19–21 Anthony Haughey, courtesy the Gallery of Photography, Dublin; pp. 30–31 John Hinde, courtesy Grayling Limited, Dublin; p. 32 Martin Parr, courtesy Magnum Photos, New York; p. 33 Elliott Erwitt, courtesy Magnum Photos, New York; pp. 36–39 Victor Sloan, courtesy the Gallery of Photography, Dublin; p. 40 bottom, p. 41, and p. 44 Philip Jones Griffiths, courtesy Magnum Photos, New York; p. 48 Seán Hillen, courtesy the Gallery of Photography, Dublin; p. 54 Paul Graham, courtesy PPOW, New York; p. 55 top and bottom Seán Hillen, courtesy the Gallery of Photography, Dublin; pp. 58–59 James Nachtwey, courtesy Magnum Photos, New York; p. 60 Donna DeCesare, courtesy Impact Visuals, New York; p. 62–63 Willie Doherty, courtesy Matt's Gallery, London; p. 64 Philip Jones Griffiths, courtesy Magnum Photos, New York; p. 65 top Abbas, courtesy Magnum Photos, Paris; p. 65 bottom Jim Tynan, courtesy Impact Visuals, New York; pp.74–75 from *Indian Circus*, copyright © 1993 Mary Ellen Mark, courtesy the Mary Ellen Mark Library, New York; pp. 76–77 from *An Autobiography*, copyright © 1993 Richard Avedon.

CORRECTIONS

On page 58 of Aperture issue #132 "Immagini Italiane," the by-line for the article entitled "The Invention of Southernness: Photographic Travels and the Discovery of the Other Half of Italy" reads: "By Antonella Russo with research by Diego Mormorio." The appropriate attribution is: "in consultation with Diego Mormorio."

The National Photography Centre
Temple Bar, Dublin, Ireland

The National Photography Centre will provide purpose-built accommodation for the three leading photography organizations in Ireland:

- The Dublin Institute of Technology School of Photography offers 3-4 year full-time training courses leading to a Technician Diploma in Photography.

- The Gallery of Photography is the only gallery in Ireland devoted to photography. It offers a flexible exhibition space for contemporary work by Irish and international photographers.

- The National Photographic Archive offers a flexible exhibition space for documentary/historical work from the National Archive's own collection and other international collections.

Facilities in the National Photographic Centre will include:
* Two exhibition galleries
* A Photographic Archive
* Geneaological research resources
* Conservation facilities
* Darkrooms
* Administrative offices
* An external projection system

This project is part funded by the European Regional Development Fund.

Architects: Group '91 Architects
Project Architects: O'Donnell & Tuomey
Client: Temple Bar Properties Ltd.
Completion date: December 1994

For further information, contact:
Una Johnston
Photography Executive
Temple Bar Properties,
18 Eustace Street, Dublin 2, Ireland
Tel: (353 1) 677-2255
Fax: (353 1) 677- 2525

The Gerald Peters Gallery

Abandoned Church Near Taos, New Mexico, 1932
vintage platinum print, 10 by 8 inches

is pleased to represent
the work of

Paul Strand

GERALD GP PETERS GALLERY

439 CAMINO DEL MONTE SOL, P.O. BOX 908 SANTA FE, NM 87504-0908
TELEPHONE 505 988-8961 FAX 505 983-2481

SANTA FE · NEW YORK · DALLAS